Library of Congress Cataloging-in-Publication Data available


ISBN 0-439-33714-3


10 9 8 7 6 5 4 3 2 1                                                    00 01 02 03 04


Printed in the U.S.A.

First printing, September 2001

# "Why do I have stinky feet?"

## ... and other

**Questions Kids Ask**™

## About Themselves

■SCHOLASTIC

New York   Toronto   London   Auckland   Sydney
Mexico City   New Delhi   Hong Kong   Buenos Aires

## QUESTIONS KIDS ASK ABOUT THEMSELVES

Dear QKA Reader,

Your body does such interesting things. Sometimes I really envy you humans! You can laugh. You can burp. You can even grow hair out of your head. Lizards can't do any of that stuff!

I have lots of questions about the human body and how it works. You probably have questions, too. Like how come your toes wrinkle in the bathtub? What happens when you sneeze? Why do people have belly buttons? (Lizards don't, you know!) And, the one question that has always stumped me: If people don't eat bugs, how can they have "butterflies" in their stomachs?

Lucky for you and me, this book will answer all those questions—and more—about how your body does all those special things.

Read on! And keep on asking questions.

Your pondering pal,

Leonardo da Lizard

P.S. I love playing hide-and-seek! I wonder if you can find my hiding places on every page of this book.

Burps start in your stomach, which is like a giant stretchy bag. As you eat and drink, food and liquids go down your "food tube," or esophagus, and enter your stomach. Some air is always in your stomach, and swallowing food displaces some of it. The air starts to put pressure on a tiny one-way valve at the bottom of the esophagus called the lower esophageal sphincter, or L.E.S. When enough pressure builds, the valve opens backward, the air escapes, and *BURP!*

You tend to burp more when you eat fast or talk while you're eating because you swallow more air with your food. During digestion, acids in your stomach react with food to produce other gases that add to the air. Drinking carbonated beverages, such as soda pop, makes you burp even more because they're full of gas.

8

# Why do I burp?

## It's your body's way of relieving pressure.

### Try this experiment:

To show why a stomach burps, you'll need: a 3-ounce disposable cup, a zipper-type sandwich bag, vinegar, and baking soda. To avoid a mess, do this experiment over a sink. Place 2 teaspoons of baking soda in the bag. Fill the cup with vinegar. Without spilling the vinegar, place the cup in the bag, and seal the bag shut. Once the bag is sealed, dump the vinegar into the baking soda. Like the acid in your stomach, the vinegar will react with the baking soda and cause a bunch of gas to be produced. The gas pressure will build up and the bag will pop with a burp!

You're laughing, eating, or suddenly get scared and—*HIC!*—you have a case of the hiccups.

You get hiccups, or hiccoughs, when something unusual happens to your diaphragm. Your diaphragm is the muscle at the bottom of your chest that helps you breathe.

Sometimes, your diaphragm misses a beat in its normal rhythm and jerks tight. When this happens, a tiny flap at the back of your throat, called the epiglottis, covers up the opening of your windpipe. This flap keeps air from going into your lungs. The result is a series of hiccups that continue until your diaphragm settles down again.

## EXTRA

Most hiccups last only a minute or two, but a few cases have been recorded of people hiccuping for days, weeks, or even years!

# What causes a hiccup?

## It's an open-and-shut case.

# What do eyelashes do?

## Blink and you'll miss the answer!

**T**wo sets of eyelashes, top and bottom, grow out from your eyelids. They perform the important job of keeping dust out of your eyes and protecting them. Your eyelashes detect the dust around you and make you shut your eyes before you've even thought about it!

Eyelashes are made of very special hairs, which are really sensory organs. Sensory organs allow you to respond to your environment using one of the senses—sight, hearing, smell, touch, or taste. Eyelashes help you get information through touch.

Human beings have very few of these special hairs. You have some around your lips, on your cheeks, in your nose, and, of course, eyelashes around your eyes.

**EXTRA**

People blink about once every five seconds. Blinking is important because it allows the eyelids to keep the front of the eyeball, or the cornea, moist.

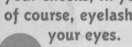

10

# What do eyebrows do?

## Hint: They don't just decorate your face.

Scientists believe that your eyebrows keep forehead sweat, snowflakes, and raindrops from falling into your eyes. This may also explain why your eyebrow hairs are slanted outward—to direct this moisture toward the sides of your face.

You also use your eyebrows, as well as your eyes and mouth, to express how you feel. Look in a mirror and watch how your face moves as your feelings change. These are called facial expressions. Pretend someone broke your favorite game. Notice that you've lowered your eyebrows into a scowl. Now imagine someone just surprised you by giving you a cuddly puppy. Most likely, you've raised your eyebrows.

Sneezing is your nose's way of getting rid of something it finds uncomfortable. Exactly what that uncomfortable thing is depends on whether the sneeze is caused by a cold, an allergy, or other irritant.

You catch cold when your nose is invaded by tiny germs. These germs make yucky stuff called mucus, which builds up in your nose. Sneezing gets rid of the mucus, but it also blasts out an invisible cloud of germs just looking for another place to live. So if you sneeze on your friend, or on something your pal then touches, the germs might find a new home—inside your unsuspecting friend!

If you have an allergy, your nose is trying to get rid of something, like pollen or dust. Your body produces histamines as a reaction to whatever is causing the allergy. The histamines cause a runny nose, sneezes, and sometimes watery eyes.

12

# Why do I sneeze?
## Your nose knows!

AHH... Choo

### How fast does it go?

| | |
|---|---|
| Sneeze | 75 to 100 miles per hour (120 to 160 kph) |
| Hurricane | 74+ miles per hour (118 kph) |
| Cheetah | 70 miles per hour (112 kph) |
| Car on highway | 65+ miles per hour (104 kph) |

# Why do I have hair in my nose?

## It's for screening, not for styling.

You take in the air you breathe through your nose. In addition to the all-important oxygen, air contains small particles, such as dust, soot, and bacteria. Your nose hair guards against this dirt so you don't breathe it into your lungs.

Your nose hairs, as well as the mucus in your nose, trap dust and dirt particles. Sometimes, the trapped particles tickle your nose and make you sneeze.

Nose hairs grow at the entrance of each nostril. These special hairs are known as cilia.

13

# What do thumbs do?

## Originally, they were a means of escape.

**H**uman hands have developed over millions of years to become the handy tools they are. Because our thumbs are located "opposite" our fingers, allowing them to touch the fingers, they are called opposable thumbs.

Millions of years ago, the group of mammals called primates developed opposable thumbs to help protect themselves from predators. Primates include: apes, monkeys, prosimians (animals such as lemurs), and humans. Opposable thumbs allowed primates to grab branches and, therefore, climb trees to avoid enemies that couldn't climb.

Imagine trying to escape from a ferocious beast by scrambling up a tree—without using your thumbs! Your thumbs give you the ability to perform many tasks, including eating, writing, computer keyboarding, and getting dressed.

# Why are people right- or left-handed?

## On the one hand, there's genetics . . .

You are considered either right- or left-handed depending on which hand you naturally use for tasks, such as pointing, writing, and throwing. Only about 10 percent of people are left-handed. The rest are right-handed.

Genetics, or the traits you inherit from your parents, may play a part in determining whether you are right- or left-handed. But scientists have had a difficult time proving this.

Social factors have also contributed to right-handedness being more common. Various cultures throughout history were suspicious of left-handedness, and some even thought it was evil. As a result, left-handed people were often forced to learn to use their right hand.

### Left Is All Right
#### Some notable left-handed people:

| | | | |
|---|---|---|---|
| Bill Clinton | 42nd U.S. president | Prince William | British prince |
| Whoopi Goldberg | comedienne | Julia Roberts | actress |
| Matt Groening | cartoonist | Mark Twain | novelist |
| | | Pablo Picasso | artist |

15

If you bump the sensitive area behind your elbow in just the wrong way, you'll feel pain shoot down your arm all the way to the tip of your little finger. As you're hopping around in pain, some helpful person might tell you that you just bumped your "funny bone," but you probably won't find it funny at all. It hurts!

Not only is your funny bone totally *not* funny, it isn't even a bone! The area of the arm that we know as the funny bone is actually the meeting point of the upper-arm bone, called the humerus, and the primary lower-arm bone, the ulna. In this soft, sensitive space, the ulnar nerve passes close to the skin. When you bump this area, the nerve is stimulated and it creates an unusual (and unpleasant) tingling sensation.

# Why is my funny bone so sensitive?

## Yeeow! Banging it isn't funny.

**Funny Business**

The term "funny bone" might derive from the name for the upper-arm bone, even though there's nothing "humorous" about the humerus.

# What's a laugh?

## It's all in the breath.

### A Laugh a Day

We laugh much more in groups than when we're alone. That's why many scientists believe laughter has become a way to express ourselves in social situations. Babies laugh to communicate. Adults laugh to bond together and relax, such as when they enjoy a joke together.

When you laugh, you chop up each exhalation, or breath out, into a bunch of short, repetitive sounds, such as "ha-ha-ha." Each sound, or vocalization, is about one-sixteenth of a second long, and the sounds come a quarter of a second apart! Certain respiratory organs and muscles, including your diaphragm, tighten up, or contract, and extra oxygen quickly enters your blood.

About 80 percent of laughter has nothing to do with humor. We laugh when we are nervous, sad, excited—or just because someone else is laughing!

Like sneezing or sleeping, laughter is something all humans do. It's a natural form of communication that humans are born with. Babies laugh when they're only a few months old. Other mammals laugh, too. For instance, excitable, young chimpanzees laugh when playing.

17

# Why do I sweat?

## It's your built-in way to beat the heat.

**S**weat, or perspiration, helps control your body's temperature. Your body likes to be at a constant 98.6°F (37°C), and it's always making adjustments to stay there. By sweating, your body releases excess heat to stay cool.

Skin contains tiny tubes, or ducts, called sweat glands. You have nearly 100 sweat glands in every square inch (6.45 square cm) of your body. There are larger sweat glands under your arms, on the palms of your hands, and on the bottoms of your feet.

Each sweat gland flows to the outer layer of your skin through tiny openings called pores. When your brain tells your body to cool off, your sweat glands produce a salty water that covers your skin. As this water, or sweat, evaporates, your body becomes cooler.

### EXTRA

Sometimes you perspire when you eat spicy food. This is caused by a chemical in the food that stimulates nerve endings in your mouth and tongue, which then send a false signal to your brain that your body temperature has gone up. This sets into motion the events that cause you to sweat.

18

Stinky feet are the result of tiny microbes that live in your shoes and eat the sweat from your feet. Our bodies are covered with microbes. We need these micro-bugs to protect us from other more harmful microbes. The problem is that when microbes feed off us, they produce waste material. That's the smelly stuff! A certain microbe likes sweaty feet. Socks and shoes trap the sweat and create a bountiful buffet for the microbes. The next thing you know—*P.U.!*

### EXTRA

The scientific name for foul feet is bromhidrosis. The cure: Wash your feet often and change your socks!

## Fragrant Footsies!

Can't stand the company of your own feet?

Soak your toes in salt water.

Squeeze a lemon on your feet.

Bathe your feet in cold water.

# Why do I have stinky feet?

Believe it or not there's something living on the bottom of your feet!

# Why is some hair curly and some straight?

## It's a chemical reaction.

The natural curliness of hair is mostly determined by the kinds of proteins that form the bonds in your hair shafts.

Hair is mostly made of protein. Proteins are made of amino acids. Some amino acids contain an element called sulfur. When proteins containing sulfur link together, or bond, the combination is called a disulfide. The more linking between disulfides, the curlier your hair will be.

Like eye color and hair color, the straightness and curliness of your hair is determined by the genes you have inherited from your parents.

### Staying in Style

Some people "perm" (short for permanent wave) or "relax" their hair to change its appearance. Perms make hair curly, and relaxing makes hair straight. In both cases, chemicals are applied to the hair that will change the way its proteins bond. When bonds are broken, hair can be straightened. When bonds are reformed chemically, hair can be curled. But neither perms nor relaxations are actually permanent. As hair grows, each strand reverts back to its natural shape.

# Why are there differences in people's skin color?

Your skin color is mostly determined by your genes. Among other things, genes determine the amount of melanin produced in the skin. The more melanin you have, the darker your skin will be.

Early humans developed different characteristics according to where they lived. Today, geography plays less of a role in determining skin color.

Although people with different skin colors may appear different, genetically we're almost identical to one another. Even within families, skin color can vary greatly.

## EXTRA

Genes also determine your eye and hair color, as well as your body size and shape.

We may look different, but we're all members of the human race.

crayons

21

# Why do people get dizzy?

You're twirling around and suddenly you feel dizzy. Why?

The inner ear has three liquid-filled loops, known as the semicircular canals. Each canal has tiny hairs growing at the bottom of it. They are connected to nerves that carry messages to your brain about the position of the hairs.

When you move, the liquid swishes back and forth, pressing against the hairs and making them bend. The brain then knows to adjust your muscles so that you can keep your balance. When you twirl, the liquid moves rapidly back and forth over these hairs. Your brain receives confusing information and can't react quickly enough. As a result, you get dizzy. Fortunately, the liquid soon settles down, and your brain gets your muscles working properly again. That's when the dizziness goes away.

**Think of it as an argument between your brain and your ears.**

## What makes you dizzy?

Illness

Performing somersaults

Riding in amusement rides

Spinning around

Standing up too fast

Sailing on rough seas

22

# What causes my ears to "pop"?

## They're under pressure . . . air pressure!

If you ride in a fast elevator, you may notice that your ears feel blocked or stuffy. And then you might hear a *crackle* or *pop* deep inside your ear. Why? Because as the elevator goes up or down, the air pressure changes. The blocked or stuffy feeling happens because the pressure outside of your ear changes faster than the pressure inside your ear. Fortunately, your ears can usually handle this pressure.

Your ear has a narrow tube called the eustachian tube, and its job is to keep the air pressure inside your ear equal to the air pressure outside your ear. Normally, this tube is closed, but when you experience a change in air pressure, the tube opens to allow air into or out of the middle ear. The *pop* you hear is the sound of your eustachian tubes opening.

## Unstuff 'em!
If your ears feel blocked, help your eustachian tubes open by:

Opening your mouth wide

Sucking on hard candy

Swallowing

Yawning

## EXTRA
At sea level, air presses against you with a force of 14.7 pounds per square inch (1 kg per square cm). The higher you go, the less pressure there is.

# What is a belly button?

**Innie or outie, it doesn't help you hold up your pants.**

Before you were born, you grew inside your mother's body. While there, you couldn't get food or oxygen from the outside world. You had to get them through a special organ called a placenta.

The placenta is a clump of blood vessels that nourishes each unborn baby. It takes oxygen and nutrients from a mother and passes them to her baby through a flexible tube called the umbilical cord, which is attached to the baby's stomach.

Once the baby is born, it no longer needs the cord. The doctor cuts off all but a tiny stump, which usually falls off a few weeks later. None of this hurts the baby at all. The belly button, or navel, is the spot where the umbilical cord had been connected to the baby's stomach.

24

# How do babies learn to talk?

## Ga-ga, goo-goo—what they say depends on you!

*Waaa!* That's the first sound healthy babies will make when they are born. Crying helps open babies' lungs and gets them ready for the world. Babies learn to make more sounds and form words from listening and watching people around them. They copy what they hear.

At first, babies use sounds we can't always understand—baby talk—to try to get what they want: food, a nap, or a change of diaper. Usually, at about six months, those sounds start to have more meaning. By the time babies are a year old, they're forming words. Talking or reading to a baby, singing songs, playing "peek-a-boo,"—all help a babies learn to talk.

### Baby Talk
**By their first birthday, most babies can:**

Recognize their name.

Understand words like "bye-bye" or "up."

Say words like "ma-ma," "no-no," "go-go."

Laugh and try to imitate the sounds you make.

25

If you have freckles, chances are good you've inherited them from your parents, just as you inherit wavy hair, brown eyes, or long legs. But freckles usually don't appear when you're born. They show up after you've spent time in the sun.

Freckles are made of melanin, a substance that gives skin its color. Melanin is produced by cells in the thin outer layer of your skin. A freckle appears when a lot of these cells clump together in one spot.

## EXTRA

Natural blonds and redheads, who are likely to have light skin, are more likely to have freckles than darker-skinned people.

# What are freckles?

## They're easy to spot, but only on certain people.

### Sun & Skin

Too much sun gives you more freckles. It can also be dangerous to your health. Here are some sun-wise tips:

- The lighter your skin, the shorter the time you should spend in the sun.
- Put on sunblock. Don't forget your nose and lips.
- Wear a hat and other cover-ups.

# What are goose bumps?
## The answer is nothing less than hair-raising!

**EXTRA**

Goose bumps on a frightened or angry animal puff up its hair and make it look bigger, scaring away would-be attackers.

**B**rr! You get out of the pool and suddenly your body is covered with tiny bumps. Why? Each hair on your body usually lies flat, sitting in a little pocket in your skin called a follicle. When you get chilly, angry, or scared, the muscles around the follicle tighten, making the hair stand up.

More than 100,000 years ago, human bodies were covered with a lot of hair. Goose bumps pushed up all of this hair, making it fluffier and fuller in order to help keep the body warm. Though people are not so hairy anymore, goose bumps still keep trying to do their job!

## What are dreams?

### Your brain is never totally asleep.

Dreams—thoughts, images, or emotions occurring during sleep—have fascinated people through the ages. Dreams are affected by things you have seen, heard, or felt.

Your dreams may include urges or interests you have. Sometimes, your dreams can be caused by your physical state. For example, if you are cold, then you might dream about being in the snow.

Humans aren't the only dreamers. Animals, such as dogs, also dream. If a dog moves its legs while it sleeps, it may be dreaming of playing "catch" with its human companion.

**EXTRA**

Generally, everyone dreams for about 100 minutes during 8 hours of sleep. There are usually 5 dream periods, lasting 5 to 50 minutes each, in one night's sleep.

**Dream Signs**

Rapid Eye Movement, called REM, is one way to tell that people are dreaming. While we dream, our eyes usually move back and forth behind our closed eyelids.

# Why do people snore?

## Sometimes, breathing isn't a breeze.

**Man, that's LOUD!**
Sound levels are measured in decibels (dB)

| | | | |
|---|---|---|---|
| Normal breathing | 10 dB | Whistling teakettle | 80 dB |
| Normal conversation at 5 feet (1.5m) away | 65 dB | Loudest recorded snore | 88 dB |
| | | Motorcycle | 90 to 110 dB |

Snoring occurs when the soft part of the roof of your mouth, the soft palate, vibrates as you inhale air. If the airways in your nose and throat are partially blocked, the speed of the air increases. The vibrations are heard as a snore.

Snoring can be caused by many different things. In an overweight person, fatty tissues can build up and block the airways. Poor muscle tone may mean that the muscles that open the airways won't work properly. Nasal problems and enlarged tonsils can also cause snoring. Any illness that narrows the airways, such as asthma or allergies, may lead to snoring as well.

Most snoring can be corrected by a change in diet and getting more exercise. For snoring caused by allergies, doctors may recommend medication.

29

# How fast do children grow?

## It's no wonder those pants are too short!

From birth until the age of four or five, children grow very rapidly. During this period, youngsters grow at a rate of about 3 inches (7.6 cm) in height per year. After the age of four or five, children grow an average of 1 inch (2.5 cm) each year until they reach their teens.

Between the ages of 13 and 15, kids usually go through a change called the adolescent growth spurt. During this time, teens experience a period of accelerated growth. Boys average 4 inches (10.5 cm) of growth per year, and girls average 3.4 inches (9 cm) per year. After the adolescent growth spurt, the rate of growth slows and eventually stops sometime in early adulthood.

Scientists who study growth do not look at the actual height a person has achieved by a particular age. They look at the difference between a person's height from year to year. Growth is measured in height rather than weight because height measures the growth of only the skeleton. Weight measures all of the body at once.

There's a formula that will estimate your adult height based on your parents' heights. Here's how to use the formula: If you're a boy, add your parents' heights together, divide by two, and then add 3 inches (7.62 cm). If you're a girl, add your parents' heights, divide by two, and subtract 3 inches (7.62 cm).

# How can I tell how tall I'll grow?

## Your current height isn't the best clue.

Humans have a circulatory system, a network of blood vessels that controls temperature and distributes oxygen and nutrients throughout the body. The dermis—the layer just below the skin's surface—contains miles of tiny, branching blood vessels called capillaries.

When your heart beats faster than normal, it pumps blood from the center of your body into the capillaries. The additional blood "flushes" your face with additional color—a blush. This can happen when your body tries to cool off on a hot day, or when your muscles "burn" more oxygen than usual because of exercise.

Blushing can also result from feelings. Strong emotions can speed up your heart rate, filling your capillaries and making you blush when you are scared, angry, or embarrassed.

# Why do I blush?

## Sometimes, your feelings are as plain as the nose on your face!

**EXTRA**

Humans aren't the only creatures who blush. Males of the Old World monkey species called mandrills (*Mandrillus sphinx*) have colorful blue and red markings on their faces and rumps. When these animals are frightened or angry, these areas grow brighter.

# Why do I yawn?

## Your brain is trying to tell you something!

You can cover your mouth, but you can't stop it from happening. Yawning is one of many involuntary reflexes. Here are three more:

- The pupil of your eye gets smaller in light.
- Your foot kicks when your knee is tapped.
- Your eyes close when you sneeze.

**EXTRA**

You're in a room, and a person yawns. Then another person yawns. Then yet another . . . What's going on? Yawning seems to be catching—but nobody knows why.

Yawning is what your brain tells your mouth to do when your body is tired. If you yawn late at night, it probably means you should get some sleep. But if you've slept well and you yawn a lot during the day, it may be a sign that your body is missing something.

To work properly, your body needs oxygen, a gas in the air. Yawning lets more oxygen in. Exercising—outside, if possible—peps up your body by bringing in a fresh supply of oxygen.

Yawning in public is thought to be rude. But you can't really stop a yawn—it's an involuntary reflex. That means you can't control it. So just be sure to cover your mouth the next time you yawn.

# What are fingernails made of?

## It has something to do with plants . . .

Fingernails are made of a protein called keratin. You absorb keratin from plants, or from the plant-eating animals you eat. Keratin forms cows' horns, horses' hooves, and your hair, in addition to your nails.

At the root of your nail is the nail bed, from which the entire nail grows. The nail bed is the only part of your nail that is alive. The part that grows out is dead. That's why cutting your nails is a pain-free process. It takes about six months for the average fingernail to grow from the base to the tip and from one to one and a half years for the average toenail!

34

# How fast does hair grow?

## It's too slow to waste your time watching.

The hair on your head grows very slowly. The average is ½ inch (1.3 cm) per month. That's only about 6 inches (15 cm) per year. Strangely, the hair that you see is actually dead. That's why it doesn't hurt when it's cut. The living part of your hair is the root, which is below your scalp and anchored in a little pocket called a follicle. That's why it hurts when you pull out a hair.

Hair is basically made up of keratin, a hard protein. As the hair is created from the root, it grows upward.

Even though you don't realize it, hair continually sheds and regrows. The average life of a strand of hair varies from three to five years. Each follicle acts independently from another so the that total amount of hair on your head remains constant.

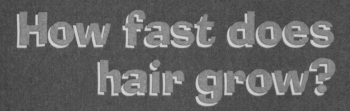

35

Whether you're soaking in the tub or paddling in the pool, after a while in water, the skin on your fingers and toes will start to wrinkle. Here's why:

The skin on the soles of your feet and the palms of your hands is thicker than the skin on the rest of your body. This thick layer is called the stratum corneum. When you soak in water for a period of time, the stratum corneum soaks up some of the water, and it plumps up. The trouble is, the expanded skin has nowhere to go. So it begins to buckle or wrinkle, and that's what gives you pruny toes in the tub.

All skin absorbs a little water when you bathe. But the stratum corneum absorbs the most, which is why you only notice wrinkles on your feet and hands.

# What makes my toes wrinkle in the bathtub?

## The same thing makes you pucker in the pool.

**Waterproof Skin**

Your skin is coated with an oily substance, called sebum, that helps keep water out.

# Why do I have fingerprints?

## They help you get a grip!

Can you recognize the markings on the tips of your fingers? The FBI divides fingerprint patterns in these ways:

**Arch**
Plain Arch: The swirls on your fingertips are circular- or spiral-shaped.
Tented Arch: Fingerprint ridges form arches that look like spikes or steeples.

**Loop**
Radial Loop: Loops spiral toward your thumb.
Ulnar Loop: Loops spiral toward your pinky finger.

**Whorl**
All of these types of fingerprint ridges are made up of circles:
• Plain Whorl
• Central Pocket Loop
• Double Loop
• Accidental Whorl: Combines a whorl and one other pattern.

In detective stories, a fingerprint often gives the criminal away. But what are fingerprints really for? Well, you use your fingertips to feel something to tell if it is smooth, scratchy, or slick. Those lines, curves, and swirls that cover your fingers and create fingerprints are more sensitive to textures and to temperature. They help provide more detailed information about whatever you're touching. You also use your fingers and hands to grab and hold things. The ridges of your fingerprints give you a better grip than you'd get with just smooth skin.

It's really hard to change your fingerprints. Mild burns or cuts won't affect the patterns. As the injury heals, the pattern regrows in exactly the same way!

37

Imagine that your eye is a hollow ball. The back wall of the eye is called the retina. It's covered with cone-shaped cells called cones, which detect the colors red, green, and blue.

Some people are born with cones that can't detect a particular color. This is what most people call color blindness. Doctors call it color vision deficiency. For instance, a person with red deficiency sees blue and green, but he sees red as a kind of muddy mix of blue and red. Blue deficiency is uncommon, but a person with it would see blue as a mix of red and green.

Color vision deficiency is an inherited trait. It's passed from parents to the child, like other physical characteristics. Color blindness is mainly passed from your mother.

**EXTRA**

Boys are much more likely than girls to be color-blind. About 8 percent of boys have some form of color vision deficiency.

# Why are some people color blind?

## It's a trait they inherit from their moms.

Paint Chips

ACME Paint Antique White

ROSE

ACME Paint Pink

ACME Paint

ACME Paint BLUE

**The World in Black and White**

If you were totally "blind" to color, you'd see the world in black and white, like an old-time movie. Although it sometimes happens, this condition is very rare. It's called *monochromasia*.

# Why do newborn babies have blue eyes?

## It takes time to develop their true color.

**Changeable Baby**

Most babies are born with blue eyes. Eye color is caused by pigments in the iris, the colored part of the eye that circles the pupils. Babies' eyes look blue or gray because those pigments aren't all in place yet. During the first six months to one year of life, a baby's exposure to light causes the pigments to appear and causes their eyes to change to their final color.

Newborns begin life with eyes that are already one-third the size of adults'! Yet even with those big, wide eyes, newborns can only see things about 6 inches (15 cm) away from their faces. As babies grow, they gain the ability to see things that are farther away, to judge how far away something is, and to follow the movement of objects.

A newborn baby's skin takes some time to develop to its final shade. It starts out pale and darkens during the first year of life. Moments after birth, a newborn often has bluish or grayish skin that turns a healthy pink after the blood circulates for a while.

39

# Why does my stomach grumble?

## It's your tummy's way of showing its muscle.

**W**hen you eat, the food you chew passes down your esophagus into your stomach. Your stomach churns up your food with acid, turning it into thick soupy stuff. This mushy mix enters the small intestine, where the nutritious parts of the food are absorbed into the body. The wastes move along to the large intestine, and eventually, they are passed out of your body.

After the food is gone, your stomach keeps churning away, like an empty washing machine. But it isn't really empty. Your stomach always contains air, which enters it when you eat or drink. That grumbling sound is the air in your stomach being tumbled around. Your tummy is saying, "I'm empty. It's time to eat!"

40

GRRRRR

### EXTRA

Your stomach is higher than you think it is! The top part is just under your heart. Most of it is behind the ribs on your left side.

When you're nervous, you have a pair of glands that secrete, or send out, a hormone called epinephrine. This hormone is also known as adrenaline.

Adrenaline prepares your body to handle stress by increasing your heart rate, raising your blood pressure, and releasing sugar stored in your liver for quick energy. Adrenaline also pumps blood to important areas of your body, such as your muscles, to help you overcome what scares you. You then feel a burst of confidence that is often called an adrenaline rush.

During the stressful moment, adrenaline "borrows" blood from areas of your body that don't need it right away, in this case your stomach. The tingling in your belly is actually blood leaving your stomach to give your body strength somewhere else. It feels like butterflies are fluttering around inside you.

# Why does my stomach get "butterflies"?

## They fly in when you're frightened.

# Why do older people have gray hair?

Gray hairs are often a natural part of growing old. Your hair gets its color from a substance called melanin, which is produced in hair follicles (the "roots" of your hair). As we get older, follicles stop producing melanin. Without melanin, there's nothing to give the cells that make up every strand of hair any color.

Technically, gray hair is not really gray: It's clear. It appears gray because light passes through bubbles of air that are trapped inside hair cells.

Some people get gray streaks when they are only in their twenties, others when they're closer to 40. Gray hair runs in families, but it doesn't automatically mean you will go gray if one of your older relatives has gray hair. Your lifestyle and environment are also believed to play a part in your hair turning gray.

## EXTRA

Most people think that gray hair is more wiry than other hair, but there is no difference in structure. The gray hair appears coarser because it has less natural oil and stands out against other hair.

## Let's get to the root of the situation.

## ― QUESTIONS KIDS ASK ABOUT THEMSELVES ―

**enaline [uh-DRE-nuhl-in]** a liquid that's sent out into your blood 'en you become stressed, causing your heart to beat faster and your od pressure to rise; also called epinephrine

**no acids [uh-MEE-noh A-suhds]** the chemical building blocks of teins, which are necessary for life

**mhidrosis [brom-HID-roh-suhs]** the name scientists use for leasant smelling feet

**illaries [KA-puh-ler-eez]** very tiny blood tubes that connect the llest arteries to the smallest veins

**[SIHL-ee-uh]** long, thin, tiny moving hairs found in living beings; you e them in your nose, ears, windpipe, and lungs

**ea [KOR-nee-uh]** the clear covering of your eyeball that covers the il and iris

**nis [DER-muhs]** the layer of skin that's below the epidermis (the outer where your nerve endings, sweat glands, and blood vessels are ted

**hragm [DEYE-uh-fram]** a muscle at the bottom of your chest that s you breathe

**lfide [DEYE-suhl-feyed]** a compound that has two atoms of sulfur another element

**[duhkt]** a tube in your body that carries body fluids

**lottis [e-puh-GLO-tuhs]** the tiny flap at the back of your throat that rs the opening of your windpipe

**ephrine [e-puh-ne-FRUHN]** a liquid that's sent out into your blood you have stress, causing your heart to beat faster and your blood ure to rise; also called adrenaline

**hagus [e-SAHF-uh-gus]** the tube that pushes swallowed food down gh your chest into your stomach

**eustachian tube [yoo-STAY-she-uhn toob]** the soft, bony tube that keeps the air pressure the same on both sides of your eardrum

**exhalation [eks-huh-LAY-shun]** to breathe out

**follicle [FO-li-kuhl]** a very tiny pocket in your skin

**genes [jeenz]** the tiny parts in your body that decide the ways in which you will be like your parents or grandparents

**genetics [juh-NE-tiks]** the study of how traits (such as body size and shape, and skin, hair, and eye color) are passed on to you from your parents and grandparents

**gland [gland]** a part of your body that makes one or more special materials that your body uses or gives off

**histamine [HIS-tuh-meen]** a material made in your body that acts to fight off whatever you're allergic to; it often causes a runny nose, sneezing, and watery eyes

**hormone [HOR-mohn]** a material in your body that's made by your glands; it controls how and when you grow and other things your body does; blood carries it to all parts of your body

**humerus [HYOO-muh-ruhs]** the long bone in your upper arm that goes from your shoulder to your elbow

**iris [EYE-ruhs]** the colored part of the eye around the pupil (the dark spot in the center of your eye)

**keratin [KER-uh-tin]** the tough material that makes up hair, finger- and toenails, horns, and hoofs

**lower esophageal sphincter (L.E.S.) [LOH-er i-so-fuh-jee-uhl SFINK-ter]** the tiny one-way opening at the bottom of your esophagus

**melanin [ME-luh-nuhn]** a dark brown or black material in skin or hair that gives it color

**microbes [MEYE-krohbz]** very tiny living things, especially ones that cause disease; they can't be seen without a microscope

## QUESTIONS KIDS ASK ABOUT THEMSELVES

**mucus [MYOO-kuhs]** the thick, slimy, slippery substance that covers and protects the inside of your mouth, throat, nose, and other body parts

**navel [NAY-vuhl]** another word for belly button; the spot where a baby's food and oxygen supply cord is connected to the mother before a baby is born

**opposable thumbs [uh-POH-zuh-buhl thuhms]** thumbs that are opposite the fingers and are able to touch the fingers to grasp and hold things

**oxygen [OK-si-jen]** a basic element without color, odor, or taste that's needed for animals, plants, and people to live; one of the gasses of the air

**perspiration [per-spuh-RAY-shun]** salty water given off through very small openings in your skin by your sweat glands; sweat

**pigment [PIG-ment]** a material that gives color to things

**placenta [pluh-SEN-tuh]** the body part in female mammals that carries food and oxygen to unborn babies; it also takes away the baby's body wastes

**pore [por]** a small opening in the skin that lets out sweat

**primates [PREYE-maytz]** such mammals as apes, monkeys, and humans who have a large brain, shortened nose, mouth, and jaws, and well-developed hands and feet

**prosimian [proh-SEYE-mee-un]** a less-developed primate, such as the lemur; they have large ears and eyes and move about mostly at night (nocturnal)

**proteins [PROH-teenz]** substances that are in all living plants and animals; they are needed to stay alive

**pupil [PYOO-puhl]** the opening in the center of your eye that lets in light; it can open and close to let in more or less light

**retina [RE-tin-uh]** the lining on the inside of your eyeball that sends pictures to your brain

**secrete [si-KREET]** to give off

**semicircular canal [SE-mee-ser-kyuh-ler kuh-NAL]** any of the three tubes in your inner ear that help with balance

**sensory organ [SEN-suh-ree OR-guhn]** a body part that carries the messages taken in through sight, hearing, smell, touch, or taste to the brain

**soft palate [sawft PA-luht]** the moveable fold that closes off the opening to your nose from the opening to your mouth when swallowing or sucking

**stratum corneum [STRA-tuhm KOR-nee-uhm]** the thicker outside layer of skin found on hands and feet; it is mostly dead skin waiting to peel off

**ulna [UL-nuh]** the bone that goes from your elbow to your wrist on the little-finger side of your arm

**umbilical cord [uhmBI-li-kuhl kord]** the cord that connects the navel of the unborn baby to the placenta of the mother's womb

**vocalization [voh-kuh-luh-ZAY-shun]** to make sounds with your voice

## QUESTIONS KIDS ASK ABOUT THEMSELVES